How to 3D PRINT MONEY

How to

3D

PRINT MONEY

Bill Decker

TABLE OF CONTENTS

Introduction

OK, you should have guessed by now that this book isn't about actually printing money.

The idea or printing money is a euphemism. Kind of an analogy. A semblance. A bit of an idiom. A turn of phrase. Poetic license. Printing money means making money. And 3D printing money is about using 3D printing technology to make money.

No, this isn't a get rich quick scheme: "3D Print Your Way to Millions!" I'm not suggesting that with some time, a 3D printer and this book you can turn yourself into a multi-millionaire and have cars, yachts and swimming pools.

But if you are in business, you will need to understand and embrace this new technology. You will need to learn how to adopt it, how to adapt it, how to harness it, how to compete with it, how to protect your firm from it, and how to profit from it. For years as an International Market Entry Specialist, my job was telling firms they need a China strategy, or a Japan strategy, or an EU strategy.

Now, firms also need a 3D Printing Strategy.

The book is loaded with different writing styles, some horrible puns, some lengthy analogies, and some hard-hitting realities. You'll also find some resources in it and, of course, some online links you can check out. If my jokes are terrible, let me know. And if you wish to contribute to the next edition, you can find me at my email address (in the back).

One additional note. There are a few chapters in the book from Josh Jacobson, also a 3D Printing enthusiast. Future editions will have more and more guest authors!

Happy Printing,
Bill

CHAPTER 1.

The Fuss Over Rust

Once upon a time, there was a factory somewhere in America that produced rust. It was in the Rust Belt and they made some kind of rusty metal object. They paid their workers a decent wage and the boss made a lot of money. They were good at making and selling rust. Their clients were happy and it was a nice business. "Everyone needs rust" was the company motto.

The town came to depend on the rust factory and the rust factory depended on the town.

When people started realizing they could get the same rusty parts made in Japan for a lot less, the customers went that direction. They contacted rust manufacturers in Japan. They started going to trade shows and meeting Japanese rust producers. They even got the US government to help them broker rust-producing deals in Japan. Firms that never cared about the Japanese started having Japanese-speaking staff and interpreters ready.

Japan got so much rust business that Japan itself started promoting its rust! Japanese rust started to enter and dominate world markets. Japanese scholars were writing about the miracles of rust management and how the Japanese could make better, faster, cheaper and rustier rust far better than Americans could. Big name American universities like Harvard started offering MBAs in Japanese rust. Japanese CEOs started to become celebrities. Photos of Japanese rust workers in uniforms doing calisthenics started appearing in American newspapers.

Many of our rust companies decided to band together and pressure their senators and congressmen to stop Japanese rust imports. They tried to tax Japanese rust. "Japanese rust is taking our jobs!" "US rust is better!" "Buy US rust!" "Rusted in America!" Economists decided that since Japanese rust was so much cheaper than US rust, if they manipulated the currency exchange rates, Japanese rust would get more expensive and Americans would return to US rust. Japan-bashing became an art form. Why make better rust when all we have to do is blame Japan?

Guess what? Even though rust cost more after monkeying with the exchange rates, Americans were hooked on Japanese rust. They loved it. They paid more for it! There was no way Japanese rust wouldn't sell in the USA.

Our fairy tale rust-belt company started asking Japanese factories to make the rust for them. "Can we outsource our rust to you?" "Can you folks get our order and get the rust on the boat within 6 weeks?" The US firms that were still in business all began outsourcing their rust-making to Japan. US firms started to realize there was no money in making rust. Selling and marketing rust.... now THAT was where the money was. After all, who knew better than Madison Avenue how to hawk rust? Who could inventory and price rust better than the Americans? After all, the Japanese rust people were forming a conglomerate. American anti-rust regulations weren't working. Accusing the Japanese of dumping rust didn't seem to work either. High rust tariffs were not helping. At this point it was really too late for America's rust companies. Americans had trust in Japanese rust.

The US government sent trade delegations to Japan to demand that the Japanese open their Japanese rust market to US rust-makers.

The Japanese rust-makers couldn't understand why there was even a delegation. "We make better rust than you, your consumers want our rust. Our consumers don't want your rust. Why are you bothering us? You don't even bother to make the rust we like! You even label your rust in English? You don't speak a word of our language and have done no research on our market!"

While we were losing American rust jobs, the Japanese were retooling their factories so that they can make more rust without labor. The Japanese factories started using rust robots to make this rust. While the Americans were blaming low-priced Japanese rust labor, the Japanese felt this argument was incorrect. Japanese rust-makers actually earned more than their American counterparts.

And the Japanese released a figure saying 55% of the industries in Japan paid their workers more than American factories paid. Cheap labor may have opened the door, but low-cost labor as a market advantage has a shelf life.

But once again, the American rust people didn't see the trend. They didn't realize that the Japanese would themselves begin to outsource to lower-cost producing countries.

By the time the US rust boys realized that they could make this rust in China even cheaper, the Japanese were already there. Hordes of middle-American white rust-sellers were getting on planes trying to source Chinese rust. But the Japanese had tied up a lot of rust production, and the Chinese were very difficult to deal with. After all, "why should we help your failing rust business when we can think about launching our own rust companies?"

Rust knockoffs started to appear in the US market. Naive Americans would hand over all of their rust blueprints to Chinese companies, only to find out that the Chinese were making similar products and selling them to the US customers. Large hardware stores had American rust on the shelves and Chinese duplicates right next to them at a much lower price. The Chinese were referred to as immoral and unethical. But the Chinese also felt the Americans were immoral and unethical. After all, Americans didn't care about China - they just wanted cheap rust. American Rust Brokers and rust-sellers started getting late and defective shipments. They suddenly realized that outsourcing their rust production to China was neither simple, nor easy. Chinese rust experts started to show up at trade shows saying they could help Americans get through the process of buying rust. Sometimes, they would take rust commissions or rust factory fees or rust set up fees. "Never trust a rust broker" became a common American adage.

It was absolutely ridiculous for a American rust-sellers to use a one-country approach to outsource its rust. What would happen if there were political or economic risks in that country? What would happen if they were rust tariffs placed on China? What would happen if a nuclear power plant had an accident near where the rust came from? The only solution was a multi-sourced rust-producing company. There were some companies that knew how to buy rust, invest in rust and put rust experts on the ground overseas. These smart firms knew how to nurture relationships with various factories in various countries; they were the ones destined to win the rust game. The companies that also knew how to export rust and sell that rust in foreign markets (thus hedging the US market) were the ones that really did win the rust game. No one really cares where rust comes from, just like no one really cares that gourmet coffees are grown in Central America. It was always about the rust-branding, the rust-marketing, and the rust label. Chinese and Japanese companies started investing in the stock of American rust-sellers. Just as Mazda bought a large chunk of Ford Motor Company, Japanese rust companies bought into big US rust.

Our little factory had to close. The big small town boss felt his clients would never leave him. But his clients also had clients. They demanded Japanese or Chinese rust. The shareholders demanded that the firms they owned bought Asian rust. "Why should we get less return on our investment because the rust factory is living in the dark ages?"

CHAPTER 2.

No Mag's Land

There was another American factory undergoing pressure at the same time - the magazine printing company. The printing industry takes words or pictures and slaps them onto paper. The owners of this company knew that Americans would never get rid of their newspapers. They knew that people want to hold a paper or magazine in their hands. The magazines were the standard of credibility. They invented news. They reported news. People paid money to read them. Advertisers jockeyed for good placement of their ads in the magazines. And authors and reporters around the world submitted stories for slave wages, even for free! Publishers of magazines got taken to lunch in exchange for printing a certain story. With the invention of public relations, a magazine could get a great deal of its "news" for free!

Magazines tried to break even or make a little money on subscriptions and newsstand sales. They made most of their money on advertisers and the reselling of mailing lists. Some magazines, like Good Housekeeping, even licensed their name out to products. Imagine the power! All a particular magazine had to do was grant permission to use its name and the owners of the magazine would get paid!

The beauty of print was the government subsidies. Government subsidies are a beautiful thing. They give free money to companies and often mask incompetence. Print companies were also getting subsidies that protected their industry. When a French perfume was sent to the USA, the perfume box was often printed in the USA. Imported Japanese and Chinese products needed their own American boxes, too. There would be no way for Japanese or Chinese firms to effectively compete in the market unless they also bought an American printing press.

When the crazy invention of the Internet hit the USA in the early 1990s, those printers knew it would never catch on. The idea of reading a magazine on a clunky, big computer was ridiculous. And everyone knew it. Just as at one point in history "everyone knew the world was flat," in the printing industry "everyone knew" that the Internet was a fad, a type of snake oil, science fiction, and not to be taken seriously. Even portable computers weighed 6 pounds and had to have power. The screen lighting gave people headaches. Batteries would die. And the power source added weight to a briefcase. The printers continued to get subsidies, play golf with their clients, and ignore the "geeks."

But then the geeks learned to sell. The champion geek announced that everyone will have their own personal website one day. He announced that printing is going the way of the buggy whip. He said computers and this new "Internet thing" will one day house all news. He postulated that computers will talk to each other and, soon, consumers will speak directly into computers. Computers and this Internet fad will become so advanced that they will require no technical knowledge, no programming skills, not even a keyboard! And still the printers laughed. How could the champion geek know anything? What was he, the richest man in the world or something?

As magazines and newspapers had to pay high wages to print-shop workers and deal with unions, the Internet was getting faster. Wires were being replaced with routers. People didn't have to wait until the nightly news or the daily paper to see stock prices, sporting scores, or hear about train crashes. The news could be searched and found, delivered automatically to the desktop, or found on one of those mobile devices that wealthy people started carrying.

When computers started fitting into a pocket and thousands of magazines, newspapers, and print shops started closing, some of the magazines got smart. The digital magazine started to appear more frequently. Magazines could hire their own geeks and put out their own news. They could convince their print advertisers to advertise in their E-magazines.

Too bad many of the newspapers were type-cast (pun).

Traditional magazines were starting to be seen as staunch and stale. Big name pillars of publishing started going bankrupt. The leading women's pornography magazine folded (another pun) because the Internet offered more pictures, even movies, and all anonymously.

The printing press seemed doomed. The magazines had choices to make; change and adapt or die. Magazine fairytales were common. The fairytale cast the evil villain (the Internet) defeating the wonderful prints (a really bad pun). We couldn't use the same villain as the rust company. It was hard to blame Chinese labor or Japanese quality for the fall of the US printing/publishing industry. No one is walking around reading Chinese comic books or Japanese homemaker magazines.

Our villain is the Internet. The handsome prints did all he could to fight off the villain. He slashed advertising rates. He offered gifts to subscribers. He even tried to kidnap some geeks of his own. But the prints couldn't fight, and in the end, evil triumphed. But the geeks (who learned to sell) had silly names like "Yippee" and "Schmookie" and had sites with millions of readers. When it became time to make video magazines, the geeks were on the front line. They convinced movie makers to put their films on this Internet thing and then convinced the whole world to put its own movies on the Internet!

Why didn't the bankrupt business magazines think of that? Why didn't they encourage the readers and advertisers to tell their stories on their websites? Since the printers were smart didn't they think to purchase these companies once they saw market share eroding? Some of these companies were listed on the stock exchange. Printers could have bought shares with great ease.

People who dedicated their lives to printing watched the industry disappear. They waited in the tower for their prints to arrive, but he never did. Sure, there are newspapers and magazines and books, but not with the clout, prestige and market share they used to enjoy.

The theme of this story is consistent. Change comes. Firms have to adapt to change and embrace it. If they don't they will go the way of the rust companies. Japanese competition did not go away; it can't be legislated out of existence. Chinese and other Asian outsourcing is not going to disappear no matter how many laws we try to pass. New technologies can augment and replace existing technologies. American companies must compete on a global level with hungry, well-funded, entrepreneurial-minded, and government-backed competitors. How many Fortune 500 CEOs speak Hindi, Chinese, Russian, or Portuguese? Does the United States of America think that those countries are going to disappear?

And the rust is history. And here comes the next challenge: 3D printing.

CHAPTER 3.

What is 3D printing? What does it do? What's the rumpus?

Additive manufacturing, is also known as 3D printing, is a high-growth emerging market that's creating lots of buzz among industry, creative, and do-it-yourself enthusiasts. Corporations have had the use of 3D printing for many years. But now the technology is getting less expensive, easier to operate, and much more versatile.

Think of a statue as an example for traditional manufacturing, which uses (for lack of a better term) subtractive methods like drilling or cutting away to create or release an object from a block of raw material. You take a block of marble and chip away until you get a statue. If the statue is metal, the excess metal is cut away and discarded. If you made the statue the way

Michelangelo did, you would see a lot of marble chips laying around when finished.

In contrast, additive manufacturing is just that "it builds an object, in three dimensions, by laying down micro-thin sheets of material in different shapes. It turns a blueprint into a product. This material is usually a liquid resin or plastic material. The material is added a layer at a time, just as ink is laid down from your desktop printer. There is special design software which communicates with the print head. The software tells the printer how and where to deliver the material. It can be very gradual, a micron at a time. Once there is enough material laid down, the end result is an actual object with 3 dimensions. A coffee cup. A building block. A can opener.

A blueprint can be found online and users can create a product with a few mouse clicks. This technology allows companies and individuals to manufacture short runs of products without much labor, shipping or manufacturing knowledge.

However, more than plastic resins can act as the "ink" in 3D printing. Today these print heads use glass, metal alloys, food products, and even body tissue and stem cells. This means we can 3D print knives, guns, body parts, glass, bones, kidneys, dental crowns, hearing aids, and so on. The list is endless. Visit http://howto3dprintmoney .com to see more and more applications of this technology.

The industry of 3D printing is becoming one of the

world's hottest and Forbes magazine estimates that the current (2013) $3 billion global market will reach $20 billion by 2015. Other experts say it will be even bigger.

3D printing is expected to knock down barriers in international business. Experts are comparing the innovation to the steam engine and it's destined to change the entire manufacturing industry. Countries with manufacturing bases are embracing it and fearing it at the same time.

Imagine being able to print out your own eye glasses! Change the frames. Make new colors. Add your brand name. Bend the lens. Add a picture of your dog. Imagine being able to do this in your living room, in a few minutes, and have the eyeglasses ready in a couple of hours!

Why can't a company make a giant printer head, put it on a big crane, and print something large, like a house? Guess what? It's happening now.

Thousands of these blueprints are already on the Internet. People can download and change the designs, or work on the blueprint while it is in the cloud. Sites like http://3dprintingchannel.com have libraries of blueprints, ready for use. Once these designs are on the Internet, anyone with an Internet connection can access them. This means some farmer in Romania can access blueprints to build a faucet for his hoses. A Nigerian merchant can make his own sneakers. A homebuilder in Bolivia can design and make a brick. A disabled person in Hungary can customize, print, or order a prosthetic foot.

Since we can print from a blueprint, we also know that we can create our own blueprints. 3D scanning can capture an image and turn the scan into a blueprint. So that Romanian farmer can scan the faucet he has and print a duplicate.

Here is a great example of how that can help anyone, right now:

The process of getting a hearing aid is often an awkward one. Beyond the psychological ramifications of admitting and confronting the need, many patients feel that the fitting experience itself is physically uncomfortable. So imagine going to the audiologist and she scans your ear with a camera. She then tells you to go have a coffee while a perfect, custom fit hearing aid is being printed just for you. While you aren't printing your own hearing aid and buying plastics and resins to do it, you are still getting the benefit of 3D printing.

Now imagine if I moved to China and lost my hearing aid. Instead of having my audiologist order one, get to a shipping office, pack it, and ship it, she sends me a drawing over the Internet. Or tells me to log into her site from the audiologist's office in China. Next, we print my custom hearing aid right then and there. No shipping (which means no lost packages), no taxes, no customs, no waiting, no incorrect sizing. This is here (pardon the pun) and now.

CHAPTER 4

3D Myths

This chapter looks at the myths of 3D printing. Radio was criticized when it began. TV was seen as the "work of the devil." The Internet was referred to as "snake oil." Every new development, going back even before the days of a "horseless carriage" was fought, critiqued, condemned, and dismissed by many. Movie buffs felt "talkies" would never catch on. 3D printing is no different. In the next chapter we will dispel many of these myths.

Myth #1: 3D Printing will never catch on because it is too technical. This technology uses specialized diagrams, complicated drawings, unusual materials, and requires an understanding of engineering, computer aided design (CAD), and computer automation. The 3D printing machines need special parts that are not easily available.

Myth #2: Most people won't do any 3D printing because they're not manufacturing people. Let's face facts. How many people even understand manufacturing? And the USA is a service economy. Most MBAs aren't studying manufacturing and the USA's expertise is in marketing. Are we really all going to have desktops and spools of plastic going back and forth on our kitchen counters?

Myth #3: 3D printing will never replace traditional assembly line manufacturing. It's much more cost effective to have hundreds of men and women lined up in a room making 1000 widgets with each production run. Didn't Henry Ford invent the assembly line because it made more economic sense?

Myth #4: 3D printers are very slow and take a long time to make one product, so who can wait? Why wait 1-4 hours for a plastic syringe to be printed when you can have a cabinet full of them, ready to go?

Myth #5: You can only make plastic junk from 3D printers. Every picture I see of 3D printing shows some plastic cup or ball. Who needs it? How many people are using mosaic spheres in our world?

Myth #6: The labor unions will never allow a "no labor" manufacturing process. These unions are powerful and have members everywhere. There is no way they will allow products to be made without their hard work and input.

Myth #7: Holders of intellectual property will get ripped off and not paid for their designs. If I can put a CAD file into the cloud, or email it to someone, why would anyone pay for it? Just like pirating movies, software, Internet news and books....no one will pay for what they can get for free.

Myth #8: Computer automated design drawings are too big, too clunky, and take too long to download. This isn't a simple word processing file, it's an entire product design. It will take up a lot of space and most of us don't have a fast enough Internet connection to get the files.

Myth #9: Most government agencies will not approve of any parts made by 3D printing. Governments have regulations which protect its citizens. If anyone with a 3D printer can start making junk and selling it, who will regulate it? Are you saying someone can print out a car part and just install it in a car? What if the part fails and there is an accident?

Myth #10: This will never be in reach of the common man. Machines are too expensive. Set up is too difficult. Supplies aren't easy to get. Some of the 3D printing is about toys and games, but other applications seem to be about bones and eyeballs and airplane parts. It can't get to all of us.

Myth #11: There is no demand for 3D-printed products. With Ecommerce, we can find anything we want on the Internet, order it, and have it in our hands in 1 day. Who is in a bigger rush than that?

CHAPTER 5.

The Myths,
"3D bunked."

Let's 3D bunk these myths. Most new technologies get pushback. The resistance comes from people who are afraid of it, who can't grasp the relevance, who don't understand new technology in general, or those who have entrenched interests in keeping the status quo. Many radio stations fought television's market entrance. The survivors grasped the new technology (TV) and added it to their portfolios. NBC has radio stations AND TV stations.

So let's 3D bunk these myths one by one.

Myth #1: 3D printing will not catch on because it is too technical. The interesting question is, too technical for who? Engineers and manufacturing technicians have always been technical people. These practitioners have been dealing with design drawings and specifications and blueprints (print and electronic) for decades, so they will clearly grasp new technologies quickly. However, the consumer will also. The "how" of 3D printing won't be interesting to many of us; we will be interested in the benefits of it. What will it do for my business, my brand, or my needs?

As 3D printing applications mature, so does their ease of use. Right now there are even iPhone and iPad apps that allow consumers to create, augment, design, and order 3D-printed specialty products by tracing their fingers over a tablet computer. The apps get easier to use and cost less and less over time. My nine-year-old can design and print her own tea cups. Too technical? Not true.

Myth #2: Most people won't do any 3D printing because they aren't manufacturing people. The best part about myths is that there can be some truth to them. In this case, the statement is true; most people are not manufacturing people. But most people are not plumbers either! Does this mean the entire field of plumbing hasn't gotten more advanced, more accessible to the consumer (look at all the plumbing parts available in Home Depot) and more user friendly? Since we as people are still going to need "stuff," we are still going to need "stuff" made. 3D printing is another way to make "stuff." Even if everyone doesn't become a home manufacturer, we are still consumers.

Myth #3: 3D printing will never replace traditional assembly line manufacturing. There is truth to this as well. Assembly lines with large economies of scale will not go away. Those assembly lines may move from country to country, but won't disappear as a methodology. But who says 3D printing has to replace it? Can't it augment it? Just as TV did not replace radio, this rapid prototyping and incredible customization will add to assembly line's capabilities. And once the small runs available through 3D printing are utilized, we can go back to the large runs to get the per unit cost down.

Myth #4: 3D printers are very slow and take a long time to make one product, so who can wait? If the 13,000 audiologists (people who fit patients with hearing aids) service clients one at a time and can manufacture on demand for each patient, then the wait is even less than ordering a hearing aid. Over and over again we hear of one-off needs for people that are satisfied by 3D printing. Let's also not forget that early computers were slow. Early Internet access was dial-up. Early cars went 15 miles/hour. This technology will get faster and faster.

Myth #5: You can only make plastic junk from 3D printers. Not true. While some experts are fighting to make 3D printers faster, others are working on using different materials to feed into the 3D printer. Currently 3D printers can work with glass, metal alloys, stem cells (to make kidneys and other body parts) food, pharmaceuticals, plastics, dental materials, photo-polymers, resins, bacteria, and the list goes on and on.

Myth #6: The labor unions will never allow a "no labor" manufacturing process. There is no need to make an argument here. Labor unions had better figure this out, and figure out how to embrace the change. We have seen countless industries tap dance their way out of labor unions' demands. This will be no different.

Myth #7: Holders of intellectual property will get ripped off and not paid for their designs. Yes and no. There is plenty of illegal pirating of audio, video, and other intellectual property. 3D printing will be no different. However, there are legal sites to download audio, video, ebooks, and other protected IP. Some of those websites are quite small but other sites are run by multi-billion dollar firms such as Amazon, Barnes & Noble, and Apple. There will always be thieves. And there will be legal, recognizable, accountable companies that house and sell 3D printing blueprints and drawings.

Myth #8: Computer automated designs are too big, too clunky, and take too long to download. This is false. Those files are 1's and 0's and are about the size of text files.

Myth #9: Most government agencies will not approve of any parts made by 3D printing. First of all, how will they know? And secondly, aren't governments more concerned with the supplier's credibility than the manufacturing process? Just like individuals and companies, governments will benefit from rapid prototyping.

Myth #10: 3D printing will never be in reach of the common man. False. Forget that 3D printers will get less expensive and more available. It isn't about the technology, it is about the benefits of the technology. So even if there isn't a 3D printer in every home, big brands like Nike and Black & Decker will be able to use 3D printing for market research, prototyping, customization, and modification. So the next time a runner buys a Nike running shoe, she may have the 3D printing benefits embedded within the product.

Myth #11: There is no demand for 3D-printed products. True, you don't hear people saying "I need a 3D printed toy car." Let's go back to what is demanded. Quick. Customized. Inexpensive. Available. Changeable. Adaptable. The demands are about the products, not how the products are made. Everybody whined about Ecommerce. And that has only risen since it hit the common market. So as long as core desires about purchasing continue in the same trend, 3D printing will satisfy some of the demands. And we haven't even talked about what companies are demanding.

CHAPTER 6.

Why This Happens Fast

Fast is referring to the adoption of 3D printing as a business and consumer tool.

It's mobile. It goes with you. It puts power in the hands of the consumer. It makes little businesses look like big businesses. It evens the playing field. We don't even know the capabilities. We don't know where the technology is heading. It opens up whole new industries. It opens markets. It builds better competition. It forces businesses to rethink their business models. It's a cottage industry and it's a conglomerate. Some of us knew about the technology for years. Some of us are just discovering it, but can already compete with the "old guard."

Of course, we are talking about voicemail here, right? No, this must be cell phone technology. Actually, wasn't this what everyone was saying about downloadable music?

Can't some nasal off-tune singer in Milwaukee, Wisconsin upload a song to iTunes and compete with The Beatles?

Actually, all the technologies below had similar reviews and commentary:

Copy machines
Fax machines
Voicemail
Cell phones
The Internet
Portable radios
Television
Downloadable music
Movies on demand
Voice over IP
Smart phones
PCs
Apps
Tablet computers
GPS devices
Mobile media

and the list goes on...

What happened with, say, copy machines? For decades large firms were the only ones who could afford them. As demand increased, copy shops started opening up (like Kinko's) and small businesses as well as consumers could get their copies at these copy shops. Then came small business and personal copiers. Now there is one on my desk that cost $99, scans, prints, acts as a fax machine, and copies in color. This all took 25 years? 3D printing has been around for about 25 years, but now the small business and consumer boom is happening. Firms, as well as individuals, can get low end 3D printers for $300. I can use an app on my iPad and make a 3D coffee mug (with my own picture on it) by drawing it with my finger. It took me 5 minutes to learn to do it. Someone technologically inclined could learn how to use this app in 1 minute. And since every kid knows how to play video games, my 9-year-old figured it out in even less than a minute. The app is free. Free!

If I had a 3D printer on my desk, I could have produced this coffee mug at home. Or with this software, people can send it to a service bureau (like a Kinko's - a print on-demand shop) and they would mail it to me. I could wait a couple of days, or a couple of hours. It all depends on what I want to spend.

We are in the "I want it now" generation. From buying downloadable music to meeting downloadable mates, the immediate downloadable generation is here. "The trend is your friend" goes the stock market adage. Well, we can see the trend here. The big question is: will you be a friend?

Now, how many personalized coffee mugs do people need? The answer: none. No one needs a personalized coffee mug with his own snout on the outside of it. But people need parts for equipment, rapid prototypes, pieces of cars, even bones and kidneys. And waiting for product (in some of these cases) could mean life or death.

OK. Why not import? It's always amazing to see people trying to import products and thinking that the process is going to be an easy one. The country of China has done a remarkable job convincing Westerners that it is easy to have goods made in China. We have bought into the dream that we can send along blueprints or drawings to some unnamed factory in Shenzhen and that our products will arrive on time, on budget, undamaged, and according to our specifications. With 30 years in global business, I've yet to meet an executive or importer who has no horror stories about the process. And after they have finally learned how to import their toys, they turn around and find knock-offs at their customers' stores.

3D printing can help change that horror story. Instead of sending drawings to China, we can send them to a printer. Instead of waiting for the boat to leave the port, we can see the products being made in front of us. Instead of worrying about knock-off products and patent violations, we can build in-house, or in a safe room. If we want to sell our custom coffee mugs to retailers, we can put samples in their hands in a few hours. Do we still need mass production? Of course. But mass production might mean 5,000 machines instead of 5,000 employees. No unions. No boats. No lost shipments. No negotiating.

Ecommerce (which critics said will never work) has increased choice, allowed small business to compete and made purchasing easier. No one really talks about the unmentioned benefit of Ecommerce; no negotiating. As we know, much negotiating occurs in business, but few really seem to enjoy it. Large firms talk about "annual pay reviews" so they can simply put off negotiating with employees for a whole year. And many Ecommerce users find that they can search, click, and buy without some salesman nattering in their ear. They like it. So, if buying without negotiation caught on, wouldn't it hold true for manufacturing? Go back to the executives who get caught in strikes, walk outs, labor disputes, sick time, leave time, maternity time, paternity time, overtime, part time, full time, and time-and-a-half. Ask those executives what their biggest headache is. Companies closed factories and off-shored production when it was too tough and too expensive to do at home. Operators at companies were fired and replaced with voicemail. Email changed the game for snail mail. And 3d printing is changing the manufacturing game.

Technology can't be legislated out of business. It can be legislated out of your business. But technology will always find an environment where it can flourish. A friend of mine was a Fortune 500 CEO. When I asked him what he did at his firms, he told me he "creates environments." That wisdom can be adopted by firms and users alike. Create the environment now for this technology.... in your business and in your life.

CHAPTER 7.

_____

Great, More Stuff

Josh Jacobson

There's so much stuff we already have; do we really need more? Of course we do, we want new stuff and we want it now!

Stuff never gets old. We need stuff, we love stuff! We always want stuff and there will always be a market to sell stuff. But making stuff sucks. Manufacturing stuff is even worse.

It's common knowledge now that any company with a manufacturing process somewhere along the value chain can get better rates on labor by off-shoring, but more often than not, at the expense of quality. Many industries have low quality standards, where sheer volume of widgets is more important, and it's not a secret that this is where off-shore manufacturing is thriving. But what about all the other stuff in the world that requires just a little bit more quality to match the consumer price tag?

Even though we love stuff, we find it's better, faster, and cheaper to off-shore stuff. That's the simple truth. But there's still a need for stuff that's not being satisfied, and that's the need for stuff right now. Instant gratification. Not only do we want stuff, but we want stuff for cheap, and, of course, we want stuff now. That last part of the equation was never possible, but today it is not only possible it's already happening.

Back in the day, the turn of the 21st century, companies would need to prototype and, in most cases, hand-carve specialized components to manufacture. This was not only labor intensive, but was incredibly inefficient. All manufacturing companies need to innovate to stay ahead of the competition, but creating new prototypes to test emerging markets was time-constraining and expensive. Sending manufacturing jobs overseas was about as popular as chopped liver and there were horror stories to be told about getting cargo containers out of Chinese ports or not being able to clear government red tape.

It's the "I want stuff now" factor that we're seeing come to market through the channel of 3D printing. It's what's been missing all this time that has manufacturers squirming, the one thing they can't provide to the consumer. For the foreseeable future, manufacturers will have the advantage of beating the 3D printer on price, but they will clearly lose the battle for instant gratification for the consumer.

Are consumers willing to pay to have their stuff now? You bet they are, and it's already happening. Manufacturers will have to adapt quickly or they'll be competing against the in-home 3D printer as they fight their traditional competitors for a lesser and lesser share of an already niche market.

If the "I want it now" factor can suddenly be satisfied, it's a game changer. Tangible, instant gratification is what we want. Missing a few Lego pieces? Why buy a new set when you can print out replacement pieces? Want to go to the park with friends and play Frisbee but don't have one? No problem, print out a whole bunch of Frisbees and invite your friends for a game of disk golf.

Madison Avenue has been long able to encourage consumers to buy stuff they don't need, now they can get them to buy stuff they don't need without the hassle of going to the store or waiting for it to ship from a warehouse.

CHAPTER 8

3D Printing Trends

If you aren't dizzy by now, think of these trends being caused by 3D printing:

There will be less "big manufactured" goods. Specialty manufacturing will take some of that industry away.

There will be less manufacturing jobs. If audiologists can print on site and on demand, what happens to the people in the hearing aid factory?

Less shipping. Instead of placing the washer in the envelope and sending it, I (or my local hardware store) can print it when I need it.

Companies will keep lower inventory levels. The big, big, big, big MBA term is "supply chain disruption." OK. That's a fancy-schmancy way of saying "I don't have to stock the washers for a 1956 Porsche."

Rapid prototyping. This term was used before. However, with the technology being more affordable, it means rapid sample orders as well. Firms can still place the order for 1 million washers to be produced in China. But I can get 1,000 washers to my biggest customer right away.

We will have parts available for older products. Now that car buff with the 1956 Porsche can scan the washer he already has and print whatever he needs.

Governments will collect less tax revenue. If we take that washer and import it from, say, Germany, it has to clear US customs and may have a tax placed on it. If I can get the blueprint online and print it in Ohio, are there any taxes?

Green. Remember Michelangelo and the marble chips? If we 3D print, we only use what we need.

We will witness the birth of a new generation of "makers." When I got my MBA, my instinct was to stay away from manufacturing. Who needs the hassle? labor problems? Environmental Protection Agency? Boats of raw materials that never get to me? Forget it. Marketing. Finance. That's the place to be. Ahhh. Paper shuffling for big dollars... that's where the smart MBAs come to. Now a new generation of smart, young "makers" are entering the workforce and a new breed of entrepreneurs is arriving.

Brand interaction. I can interact with the eyeglass company's website and make my glasses the way I want them. The company can handle the printing. The eyeglass firm can still use Ecommerce and overnight shipping. But the consumer can augment and customize.

Controversy. When jobs disappear, people get upset. When guns can be printed by anyone with a 3D printer, people get scared. When you can print body parts (known as bio-printing) people get uneasy. When a 12-year-old can scan and copy a product, people get suspicious.

Convenience. "I want it now." OK.

Better customer service. Anyone trying to sell me something "standard" or "off the shelf" had better differentiate herself with something like lower prices, more convenience, and be willing to carry my bags of parts to my car. (Maybe even my house).

Cheaper. The machines will get cheaper. The materials will get cheaper. The websites featuring the industry will charge lower prices. The products that aren't 3D-printed will get cheaper.

Faster. The machines will get more and more advanced. They will print with greater speed.

More variety. Unless I'm wrong and everything goes back to communist grey, everyone will have more choices of their printed materials.

Complex is free. When you Google pictures of 3D printing, you see these mosaic designs and intricate plastic pieces. It takes just as much effort to print those designs as a single slab of plastic - that is, none. Who needs complicated mosaic see-through plastic pieces anyway? How about recipients of a medical implant? When body tissue can grow inside the holes of one of these implants, the body is less likely to reject it.

So, how do we 3D print money from this information? Pick the trends that your firm can embrace. Improve customer service. Focus on a consultative approach with your existing customers. Realize the competition is there, whether you outsource to do it or not. Don't buy too many machines, because the price keeps going down.

Now, let's look at the biggest trend. International Adoption. That's the next chapter.

CHAPTER 9

3D Printing and International Business

As the uncle of 3D printing, I'm entitled to my opinion. The whole world is talking about 3D printing and many of us are starting to believe that the United States will not dominate this reinvented industry.

There are many reasons for this. The first is the litigious nature of the United States. The initial thought on legal matters is that the United States seems to have more lawyers and lawsuits than the rest of the world combined. This isn't a good or a bad thing, just a thought that when looking at the USA, the high probability of litigation can offset the notion that the USA is the "world's largest market."

There's an old lawyer's joke:

> If you buy a can of dog food and your dog eating it gets sick, whom do you sue?

The answer? Everybody.

Let's look at the case of the dog food. The retailer will be sued, the distributor will be sued, the manufacturer's representative will be sued, and the manufacturer will also be sued. There is even a possibility that the ad agency (that made safety claims) could be sued - all by the person with a sick dog.

Then, of course, you've got United States government, which would regulate the dog food industry in many ways; quality of food, what is said on the label, how it is packaged, and the adherence to packaging information and expiration dates.

So let's take this scenario in the case of 3D printing.

Imagine if somebody were to print out a washer for a vacuum cleaner at the local hardware store. The store prints it out and the customer puts this washer in his vacuum cleaner. The vacuum cleaner blows up and hurts somebody. I know this is a ridiculous scenario, but it could happen - or the vacuum cleaner simply burns the rug or perhaps it catches fire.

Well, the customer is not a licensed installer, so clearly he doesn't necessarily know what he is doing. So goes the presumption. Should he have had that special washer in the first place?

However, the hardware store may not have printed this correctly. Did it have the correct printing materials? Was the technician who printed this washer properly trained? Then, one has to examine where the hardware store got the washer design. Take it a step further and start to look at the source of where that blueprint or design drawing was housed. Were the drawings in any way compromised? Was it purchased or were royalties paid? What website was it? Was it the equipment manufacturer's website or was it a third-party website selling the washers? Did the manufacturer put the drawings up correctly? Were there glitches or unforeseen circumstances that they simply did not address? So, if there were an accident with this vacuum cleaner, it would be a whole slew of people that could be sued.

This is nothing new in the USA. People buy insurance for this and large companies retain lawyers. However, small business people may not know about this insurance or they may not be able to afford it. They may have purchased the wrong policy and if they have to retain legal staff, they may choose not to get into the business at all!

Protecting oneself legally and making sure our businesses are insured drives a lot of US business decisions. Therefore people may choose to ignore the entire industry because they're not properly insured. If firms just believe their general liability insurance will cover them, they may be wrong and have to have pay increases in premiums. Often, firms need several types of insurance.

The idea of the United States' legal system is to protect the citizens. But we all know of the many times that system has been abused. Naturally, we don't want defective parts in our electronics. We clearly do not want auto parts and aircraft parts that aren't genuine. This isn't a value judgment. It's really just a business decision for a lot of entrepreneurs and other firms. So will this go overseas? Yes. When you ask insiders, many tell you that The Netherlands is the world leader in this technology. Why?

The second reason the USA may not be the hub of the industry is that ultimately 3D printing (as far as the designs and drawings) will be a traded product. Someone uploads the blueprint to a website, the website houses and markets that blueprint, and someone else downloads it or prints it from the cloud. The middleman website is functioning like a commission-based trading company. It doesn't worry about the source and the customer use; it collects designs, distributes designs, and collects money.

The Dutch are the world masters in this type of business. And right now The Netherlands is ahead of the USA in 3D printing.

The third reason that the USA may not get the pole position in the industry is that companies that rely on expensive labor will embrace the technology faster.

In much of Europe, the labor laws make it difficult to fire people, painful to cut wages in hard economic times, impossible to eliminate health insurance, and completely unacceptable to slash or deny benefits. The "social cost" of doing business in Western Europe already keeps many manufacturers out of the labor pool. Strong government subsidies often are necessary to lure firms into Europe. In the USA, employers often enjoy "employment at will" status, meaning the will of the employer. In lay terms an employer can hire someone and fire him or her the next day, with no benefits, no compensation, no reason, no birthday card, no cake.

In Europe, many employees cannot be terminated. And if employees are terminated, they still often receive a high percentage of their paychecks and all of their benefits. That's part of the definition of socialism.

With 3D printing, an employer can have a machine do a person's job. The machine doesn't get sick. The machine doesn't require five weeks' vacation. The machine can run 24 hours per day and can be moved to another region or country without disrupting an employee's family. 3D printing offers a way to manufacture close to a client's location as well as market opportunities that aren't hamstrung by labor costs. European manufacturers will run to this technology.

The fourth reason the USA may lose the competitive edge is the copycat "we don't care about your stinking patents" nature of many third world countries. The third world has been hungry too long. And the low entry-cost of this technology, coupled with Ecommerce, allows millions of hungry entrepreneurs to design and print their own products or knock off someone else's products.

Some guy in Lithuania printing a few iPhone cases may not mean much to us, but to him it could be an entire family's income. Multiply that by a few million, or a few hundred million. Compare that to a country like the

USA, which throws out more food than it eats.

So how do we 3D print money from this information?

For starters, if we are selling stuff, let's make sure our products, our literature, our promotions, and our specifications are international in standards and in language - that is, multilingual.

When we invent something, let's ask the question: where are we going to sell it?

When we look for labor, let's remember we are drawing from an international labor pool.

Hedge the US market. We don't know when the legislative hammer is coming down.

Set up banking so that we can take payments from other countries.

Have internationally-focused people in the room during R&D, strategic planning, and marketing meetings.

Think of high labor-cost markets as clients.

Remember a phone case is not a phone case is not a phone case. Different markets have different product-localization needs.

And this is just the beginning. Build this idea of international markets and labor into your strategic plan, which is discussed in the next chapter.

CHAPTER 10.

Build a 3D Printing Strategy

Did you really think you were going to read this book without having to do any real work? Strategic planning services are something many of us sell to companies. Few firms really like to buy it, though. Most firms and executives would rather have someone else write their firms' strategy. And then nothing ever happens. I call that a "bookshelf strategy." It isn't the money that stops executives from pure strategic planning, it's the time needed to do it correctly. And if executives and owners don't build their strategies, they don't buy in to the strategies.

From the book Without A Strategy:

> Without a strategy we are lost.
>
> How do we even know if we've "won?" If we don't have a target and clear definable, measurable ways to hit our target, how can we determine our own

success? In three decades I've had the chance to see firms try to build new products, enter new markets, acquire firms and reduce operational overhead all without a strategy. And I've seen many firms fail because of it.

As a management consultant, executives have asked me to build budgets without a strategy.

As an investor, I've heard pitches from firms who want funding. They've presented slide shows without a strategy.

Why do companies work without a strategy? Simple. Executives are afraid that by planning a strategy, there will be more work. Nothing could be further from the truth. A strategy (or set of strategies) will refine and define activities. If activities aren't on the strategy, they should be avoided. It's a classic case of an overused phrase: work smarter not harder.

At the end of this book, you'll find some audio links on strategic planning, and where to get a strategic planning workbook. Meanwhile, you owe it to yourself (and your firm) to start looking at the 10 key strategic issues:

What are the three biggest opportunities created by 3D printing?

-

-

-

What are the three biggest threats that 3D printing poses to my business?

-

-

-

Are my top three competitors engaged in 3D printing? How?

-

-

-

What are the three things I personally need to learn about 3D printing?

-

-

-

Why will my customers use 3D printing?

-

Why will my vendors use 3D printing?

-

How much of my time will 3D printing cost me?

-

How much of my time will 3D printing save me?

-

If we started using 3D printing in our business today, what would we tell people about it?

-

If I am a manufacturer, how will my firm compete with 3D printing?

-

That little dash (-) after each question is for the reader to fill in an answer. If you have a hard copy of this book, write on it. If you have an ebook, you may have to write on a separate paper. But if you don't write it down, right now, you are delaying. Remind yourself how TV stations hid from the Internet, how Kodak hid from digital photography, and how CD producers hid from digital music.

The last question is a trick question, in a sense. (How will my firm compete with 3D printing?) If that's the mindset after all this reading, then I have failed. Ask for your money back. (Our return policy gives you 30 seconds to return this book for your money back, or you may contact our call center in Minsk.)

If you are a manufacturer, you should have learned your lesson from the Asian market share grab; find a new way to differentiate yourself.

You can differentiate on price.

You can separate yourself based on service.

You can distinguish your firm by attractive financing.

You can adapt a consultative view of your client's

business and try to understand their whole business, including their problems.

You can introduce your clients to other market opportunities.

You can assist customers in their sales processes.

You can even produce a better product.

You can also try playing golf with your client and telling her "this fad will never catch on."

All of these bullet points are strategic initiatives. You may need several of them to set yourself apart from the technology.

The point being made here is to incorporate this new technology into your business. If you were a catalog printer in the 1980s and saw the boom of offshore printing, you could have harnessed that power. You could have told your million-catalog client that it will be cheaper in China, but less reliable and more time-consuming. The smart play? There was a hybrid - short more expensive runs of printed catalogs for immediate demand and Chinese back rooms for the large orders.

When I spoke to a large telecommunications conference, 5,000 Americans whined to me about outsourcing in India. They all worried about their jobs. My questions to them were: "How many of you speak Hindi?" "Wouldn't you be valuable to your employer if you embraced this trend and became an expert at it?"

Speak Hindi now.

Don't dwell on the last question on the list, dwell on the first one. Look at the opportunities and list how your firm will get into the game. Spend your time in that frame of mind. But if you really feel you need to compete with progress, then read the next chapter.

CHAPTER 11.

Protect Your Brand

There are two hitchhikers on the road. One is holding a sign that says "Denver." The other one is holding a sign that says "Denver, so I can meet my mom for dinner."

The second hitchhiker is more likely to be picked up. He hasn't provided information to the world, he has provided an emotion. Branding is the emotional relationship between your firm and its prospects and clients. The emotion is everything.

Take an example of a woman needing a washer for her faucet. With 3D printing, she can go online, get a diagram of the washer and print it at home. If she doesn't own a 3D printer, she can call her local hardware store, which will produce it for her. No shipping company (or shipping clerks) involved, which also means that companies relying on these shipments for survival will have to change models and rebrand.

If our "washer-needing" woman above can simply print out a faucet washer, why can't she print out a different, more competitive, and less-expensive version? She'll stick with her original brand only if it makes financial and emotional sense. Ultimately she will get to make that choice, in real time. She'll print it herself only if that's a better alternative than having it shipped or seeking it at the hardware store.

Branding services often are pitched as building a brand: the logos, messaging, colors, and corporate identity. There is a lot of chirping about fonts, typefaces, paper stocks, and company slogans. The best branding experts are familiar with all types of media: TV, movies, radio, web, social, print, email, and mobile. They toss around terms like "YouTube channel" and "Facebook page" but the pros know that those are just tools, not the essence of branding.

Less often, though, do we hear about protecting a brand. Branding should be ongoing, fresh, informative, and captivating. Firms wishing to protect their brands will spend more money more frequently. Just like in a marriage (with the emotional connection), the branding relationship needs constant attention. How many husbands know their wives love them? And how many still want to be shown and told about this love? How frequently? Let's take that a step further. That same wife may (hopefully) love her mother, her child, her cousin, her sister, her best friends, and her cat. Well, maybe she hates her cat. Does she express love the same way to all of those parties? Does she use different emotions, different messaging, and different behaviors to demonstrate this? Yes, she uses different tactics - and she does so intuitively.

So, how do we 3D print money from this knowledge?

Protecting a brand is as much psychology as it is art. A "branding salad" has many ingredients: staying in touch with clients and making new offers to them plays a role. Helping clients solve problems is a part. Offering the carrot (a pun that worked) to stay with the supplier is an ingredient. Acknowledging the client's needs is involved. Keeping the image, the lifestyle, the ideology alive keeps the client engaged and eating the salad. When you think of brand protection, think of Coke and Starbucks, which sell a lifestyle and an identity - not soda pop or coffee.

When we build brands, we need to build them with the 3D printing trends in mind - variety, speed, convenience, global reach, and brand interaction, to name a few (as mentioned in chapter 8). This can come down to the right message(s), social media presence(s), and even the company colors.

And please, do this for me. The next time you want to label a product or a company, ask a Chinese person and a Mexican person if they can pronounce the name you are thinking of. Walk into a dim sum place or a burrito stand if you can't find them in your circle of friends. These may be your customers someday. They will be your customers if you think about branding to them.

Put them into your branding salad.

CHAPTER 12.

Neo-manufacturing

Josh Jacobson

Neo-manufacturing is a new way of building goods. Factories are no longer needed in an age where similar products can be built on demand and just in time with 3D printers.

The manufacturing playing field has come a long way over the past 30 years. Using the tools of 3D printing, laborers can now arm themselves with a serious manufacturing capability. And that changes everything.

Will 3D printing really become the new concept of manufacturing? Since most labor intensive manufacturing jobs have been off shored, we're experiencing a sense of loss not only in our job market, but also in our pride and our can-do attitude. How did this come to be? Wasn't the free market economy supposed to reward those who capitalize on efficiency?

Though the short term economic hardship was brutal for some, it wouldn't be a stretch of the imagination to argue that off shoring manufacturing jobs could be one of the best things to have ever happened in the history of capitalism. We're starting to see what's really happening and it's a continuation of Adam Smith's ideas of the divisions of labor on a global scale.

By transforming laborers into innovators, 3D printing has redefined what it means to manufacture. It used to be that labors needed to show up for work at a factory, crank out widgets on their machines, day in, day out. We panicked once we saw all these manufacturing jobs being lost to parts of the world that employed cheap labor and we cried foul, kicking and screaming.

Will manufacturing jobs ever return? Probably not, if you define manufacturing the way we did in the 20th century. Neo-manufacturing, on the other hand, is just taking off. Neo-manufacturing is building what you need, when you need it and a scale that makes sense.

There are no labor laws or regulations or unions impeding the efficiency of Neo-manufacturing. It's not too far into the future that we could imagine that a child could manufacture a few Lego pieces on demand. Or a car with a flat tire or a leaky hose could identify and repair itself. Traditional manufacturing has been replaced and we should embrace the change.

When the textile industry revolutionized and improved upon the cotton gin, it spelled bad news for Eli Whitney and those who relied on his invention for their livelihood. The mentality at that time was to either adapt or be left in the dust.

We're seeing a similar transformation happening now. The entire manufacturing sector as we know it may already be outdated. Neo-manufacturing is putting the building capability once held by large factories into the hands of an individual innovator. Having a tangible product to showcase and bring to market used to be the hardest part. Now, a product can be printed, photographed and slapped on a website to test its demand and if there's someone to sell it to, a new entrepreneur is born.

CHAPTER 13.

Meaningless Research

This is called meaningless research for many reasons.

First of all, because of the "cottage industry" nature of it, we don't really know how many products some "maker" in Burkina Faso is printing out. And even if we did know, are we looking at dollars he spent or dollars he received selling products?

Secondly, since much 3D printing is used to make spare parts or designs, there may be no transaction at all once the object is 3D printed.

Third, how do you use this information? If you figured out which of the sites or research firms you trusted and got a statistic such as "this is a $2 billion market," what would you do with that information? Buy stock? Buy a 3D printer and start making checkers? Close your factory? Open a factory? The information lacks a certain call to action. Much of that call to action is to give the industry attention. If you have read this far, then you have given the industry attention.

If you are buying parts, well, maybe now that you know the 3D-printed parts market is growing, you can ask your supplier about it. Maybe you are just more informed at your company so that you can keep your job.

Fourth, research is like milk. It has an expiration date.

Fifth, imagine if someone wrote a book on the new television industry in 1945, before Uncle Miltie (Milton Berle's own TV show.... for those of you under 90) appeared on the air. When Milton Berle's show, Texaco Star Theater, hit the airways, television set sales more than doubled, reaching two million units in 1949.

Imagine if someone tried to predict what would happen with that Internet thing, back in, say, 1989 or 1990. This adds to the meaninglessness of much of the research.

Sixth, every market research jock can tell you he or she is capable of conducting customer focused research. They might ask hypothetical questions such as "if there was a 3D printer available in your office, would you use it?" People might even say "yes." But there is a long way between saying yes to a researcher and committing hard dollars and resources to making a purchase. The term "focus group" is often used in market research. The problem of course, is that group has been "focused" by someone. And with any new launch or re-launch of technology, we might not know who our likely customers are. Better to do an "unfocused group."

Below are some excerpts taken from various research sites on the Internet.

"... The 3D printed part market had a $777 million base in 2012, with 3D printed prototype parts in aerospace and automotive applications totaling $315 million and $428 million, respectively, accounting for more than 95% of aggregate sales. By 2025, the market is projected to grow to $8.4 billion, representing a compound annual growth rate (CAGR) of 18%, with transportation prototyping continuing to own a meaningful $4.0 billion although dropping to only 48% overall share as less mature sectors pick up the pace. Specifically, medical markets will soar to $1.9 billion in 2025 from a mere $11 million in 2012. Arcam first received FDA approval for its titanium orthopedic implants (initially knee and hip replacements) in 2011, while OPM only received such approval for PEKK facial and thoracic implants in Q1 2013..."

"... China may be seeing revenues in the 3D printing sector that will be as high as $1.6 billion by 2016. The estimate comes from Luo Jun, CEO of the Asian Manufacturing Association and it means China will have over one-third of the worldwide market in 3D printing. It also means China could be leading the worldwide 3D printing market in three years...."

"... China has been investing in 3D printing and additive manufacturing since 1992. Among the investments are 3D printing courses at universities..."

"... STOXX launched a Global 3D Printing Tradable Index in April. The index was launched with 10 holdings, and will totally represent 30 companies that generate revenues directly from the 3D printing sector. The new Stoxx Global 3D Printing Pure Play Index will have also 30 constituents but it is designed for bigger companies - so only nine companies are qualified to be included in the new index..."

"... Materialise, a Belgian-based pioneer in Additive Manufacturing software and solutions, combined with an award-winning Malaysian fashion designer. The results are a spectacular marriage of technology and fashion, as evidenced in Asia's very first 3D printed fashion show on June 14, 2013..."

"... The 3D printing industry is expected to continue strong double-digit growth over the next several years..."

"... Yamada Denki, Japan's largest discount consumer electronics retailer announced today that it has teamed up with Iguazu, a member of JB Group and one of Japan's largest tech companies to enter into 3D printer market..."

"... MakerBot its at a 17% market share, and has sold 13,000 printers to date. This means the total sales of 3D printers are around 70,000 units. How many consumer 3D printers have been currently sold? Somewhere between 32,000 and 70,000..."

"... Though additive manufacturing, most commonly referred to as 3D printing, has existed in the marketplace for decades, in recent years its popularity and demand has skyrocketed, turning this once little-known process into a booming billion dollar industry..."

"... The market for 3D printing in 2012, consisting of all products and services worldwide, grew 28.6% (CAGR) to $2.204 billion. This is up from $1.714 billion in 2011, when it grew 29.4%. Growth was 24.1% in 2010. The average annual growth (CAGR) of the industry over the past 25 years is an impressive 25.4%. The CAGR is 27.4% over the past three years (2010â€"2012)..."

"... Growth of the low-cost (under $5,000) "personal" 3D printer market segment averaged 346% each year from 2008 through 2011..."

I'm not sure what to do with a lot of these facts and figures. My favorite is when you hear quotes about China, as if that were a person or a department. Do we pick up the phone and call up China and ask her to buy some machines? Do we ask China if it prefers red machines to blue ones? Without identifying a customer with real needs, how does the research help (beyond telling executives who is in the industry, who the players are, and if the use is increasing or decreasing)?

Of course, these generalizations are as meaningless as much of the data.

CHAPTER 14.

Jumping In

Josh Jacobson

Be smarter than you were when the internet first came out – the opportunity to jump into an emerging industry that is primed to explode

There's never been a better time to get involved in the 3D printing industry. It doesn't matter if you know nothing about it, if someone tapped you on the shoulder in 1993 and gave you all the knowledge of how much the Internet would impact our lives twenty years later, how would you use that knowledge?

The Internet itself is still in its infancy. The way we live, the way we do business – it's all been completely changed from only one generation ago. The exponential speed at which our world is changing may be hard to comprehend. But for those who get it, making sure their positioned at the dawn of an industry will become tomorrow's Bill Gates and Mark Zuckerbergs.

There are a few reasons why such opportunity exists right now. One of which is upcoming expiration of key patents. Patents held by large companies have been stifling the potential of the 3D printing industry more than they have been promoting it. The good news is that in early 2014, several patents that prevent competition for advanced 3D printers will expire. One of these technologies protected by soon to expire patents creates high-resolution outputs in three dimensions at incredibly low costs.

This technology is called laser sintering – it's what all the hype is about and it's coming to a neighborhood shopping mall near you soon. This technology requires no special tooling and can produce cheap metal parts of nearly any size in a matter of hours. Think of the ramifications, anything that metal is used for today can be 3D printed. Add synthetics and plastics into the mix and suddenly you can image how much of our world is already made up of metals and plastics. From office chairs to bicycles to rice cookers, it seems that the imagination is the limit on what functional products can be created in an infinite number of design shapes and forms.

And then there's synthetic nylon, which can be printed into clothes or couch covers or even wallpaper. How will the $350 Billion luxury clothing industry respond to their core market making their own custom clothes whose designs are simply downloaded and printed? And when the clothes go out of style or its time for a new wardrobe, why recycle the material and reprint it into a new form?

Printing jewelry has already become a top selling market for amateurs in 3D printing. Once prices begin to drop for other building materials, we'll see more functional art being worn until wearing full blown 3D printed clothing will become the norm.

Want 3D printed shoes? You are too late, people already have them. But that should serve more as a wakeup call than missing the starting gun.

There's no time like the present and as key patents are set to expire and prices for 3D printers continues to drop, there is no doubt that creative innovators will find functional uses for 3D printed material that will shock us and revolutionize our lives in an eerily same manor the internet changed our lives just twenty years ago.

Chapter 15.

Insider Conclusions

What can we conclude from this book? How do we 3D Print money? As insiders, we have interacted with numerous people who all have their own conclusions. Their conclusions. Their movie. But each reader has to look at this technology and worry about his/her own conclusion. Our conclusions include:

Growth
We can conclude that this industry will continue to grow. Some say it will double within 5 years, other say it will quintuple. But we know that the use, applications and adoption will rise while prices get lower.

Speed
These machines will have to make stuff faster. Compare it to bandwidth on the Internet.

Variety
More and more materials will be used. While writing this

book I saw a story about a firm that 3D prints things made out of chocolate.

<u>Global adoption</u>/possible overseas lead:

Countries with high labor costs will eat this technology with their morning coffee. It's a natural in countries where good people are hard to find and bad people are hard to fire.

<u>Third world use</u>

Look for countries that can't get stuff. They'll make stuff.

<u>Revolution</u>

Laborers will change, factories will change and manufacturing as we know it will change. The idea of producing goods in one central location will be termed archaic and we'll see more and more "factories" fit into homes and businesses.

<u>Bio-printing</u>

Why wait for a kidney donor on a 2 year waiting list when a customized, functional kidney can be printed in just 2 hours?

<u>Opportunity</u>

It's all about positioning; we're at the dawn of an era and there's no time like the present to get involved.

<u>Applications. Applications. Applications</u>

More and more ways to use this technology will abound

And of course, your conclusion is….?

3D Printing Comics!

Can we remember to have a little fun?

How many CEOs complain about babysitting employees?

Inventory and warehouse maintenance were issues firms faced.

Many opened factories even
though they shouldn't have...

Most people have no patience for
managing the shop!

Employee theft or inventory control?

Not every employee has a sense of ownership!

Supervisors and foremen have also been known to be challenges.

No one wins when there is a strike...

Outsourcing to other production firms can be difficult.

And sometimes vendors can miss deadlines.

And does anyone really know how to do a factory inspection?

Of course, international off-shoring has its own difficulties.

Culture and language can be obstacles...

Each industry has its nuances.

It's hard to get firms to adhere to your schedule.

Suppliers can have different priorities than their clients.

Shipments can be delayed.

Sometimes the difference between truth and lies can seem confusing...

It's common for negotiators to present themselves in the best possible light.

As with any business, outsourced manufacturing has its difficulties.

Protecting intellectual property is a concern when outsourcing.

There are many firms that claim they have "China knowledge"

When client satisfaction is at risk, firms often get desperate...

Tempers have been known to escalate in complex situations.

It's often difficult to see who is at fault in complicated relationships.

Sometimes firms choose an indirect way to problem solve.

Freight forwarding is both an art and a science.

Environmental and worker protection becomes everyone's responsibility!

No one wants to work in an unsafe area.

And companies get more involved with supplier safety...

Firms get more "hands on" with suppliers.

Counterfeiting and knock-offs were always problematic.

Offshore management was still a mystery.

There is a special knack to managing factory workers...

Trust is an important issue!

Many so-called "China Brokers" appeared on the scene.

And people made global outsourcing appear easy...

Firms who didn't understand importing got into the business anyway.

Preserving and managing capital is critical to business.

Back room operations at companies still need close monitoring.

Each country has its own business methodology.

Suppliers became more and more aggressive as firms became dependent.

The language of manufacturing became more and more complex.

It's hard to do business through intermediaries.

Many suppliers tried to keep their clients ignorant.

And 3D Printing firms mentored one another.

Customers of all ages demand customization!

Useful Links:

http://howto3dprintmoney.com is about the book, where to get more of them and continuous link updates.

http://3dprintingchannel.com is a source for news, policies, videos, podcasts, events, companies, 3D printing designs and technology. It is the voice of the 3D Printing Industry.

http://3dchamber.com is the largest trade association in the 3D Printing Industry.

http://3dprintingpodcast.com is a free podcast (also available on Itunes and other podcast sites).

https://www.smashwords.com/profile/view/lessonsfromt heroad is Bill Decker's author page, where his other books are also found. There you can also find Without A Strategy; The Strategy Planning Workbook.

http://billdecker.com takes you to Bill's personal website and links.

www.ingramcontent.com/pod-product-compliance
Lightning Source LLC
Chambersburg PA
CBHW070821180526
45168CB00002B/701